MACHIAVELLI

BULLET GUIDE

Hodder Education, 338 Euston Road, London NW1 3BH

Hodder Education is an Hachette UK company

First published in UK 2012 by Hodder Education

This edition published 2012

Copyright © 2012 Robert Anderson

The moral rights of the author have been asserted

Database right Hodder Education (makers)

Artworks (internal and cover): Peter Lubach
Cover concept design: Two Associates

British Library Cataloguing in Publication Data: a catalogue record for this title is available from the British Library.

10 9 8 7 6 5 4 3 2 1

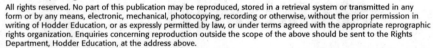

The publisher has used its best endeavours to ensure that any website addresses referred to in this book are correct and active at the time of going to press. However, the publisher and the author have no responsibility for the websites and can make no guarantee that a site will remain live or that the content will remain relevant, decent or appropriate.

The publisher has made every effort to mark as such all words which it believes to be trademarks. The publisher should also like to make it clear that the presence of a word in the book, whether marked or unmarked, in no way affects its legal status as a trademark.

Every reasonable effort has been made by the publisher to trace the copyright holders of material in this book. Any errors or omissions should be notified in writing to the publisher, who will endeavour to rectify the situation for any reprints and future editions.

Hachette UK's policy is to use papers that are natural, renewable and recyclable products and made from wood grown in sustainable forests. The logging and manufacturing processes are expected to conform to the environmental regulations of the country of origin.

www.hoddereducation.co.uk

Typeset by Stephen Rowling/Springworks

Printed in Spain

MACHIAVELLI

BULLET GUIDE

Robert Anderson

To my lovely, witty and not at all 'Machiavellian' Edinburgh friends –
Gareth, James, John, Mark, Norman, Rob, Ross, Scott and Tom – and to
the continuation of our very own Orti Oricellari.

About the author

Robert Anderson is a freelance teacher, writer, editor and translator. He
studied modern languages at the University of Exeter and went on to live
in France for a number of years.

He has taught in schools in France and the UK and has worked in
educational publishing for more than a decade. He has written a wide
variety of children's and adult's books, including a series of books on
design icons for London's Design Museum, as well as online courses for
the Tate Gallery.

Contents

Introduction

The Italian Renaissance thinker Niccolò Machiavelli has a **poor reputation** – at least in the Anglo-Saxon world. Wasn't he that chap who thought it was okay to be bad, to lie, to murder even, if what you got in the end was a good result … who argued, to put it bluntly, that 'The ends justify the means'? Wasn't he even *personally* quite a wicked man – ruthless, cunning, hypocritical? Didn't Shakespeare base his blackest villain, Richard III, on this vilest of Florentines?

Such prejudices aren't helped, either, by the fact that the very adjective '**Machiavellian**' is applied to every kind of underhand behaviour – and most especially to that of politicians.

It turns out, of course, that the **real Machiavelli** was in fact a rather different character: an able, shrewd and **honourable civil servant**, an **Italian patriot** who loved his native city, a **witty and loyal friend**, and, above all, one of the sharpest and **most revolutionary thinkers of the Italian Renaissance**. A giant, in short, even in a period that swarmed with giants. Even Machiavelli's most famous work, *The Prince* – the one that really shocked his contemporaries and which still has the capacity to shock to this day – is a rather different and rather more subtle book than its reputation as the 'handbook for tyrants' would suggest.

Machiavelli's **massive contribution** to the evolution of political thought might be summed up like this: he swept away speculation into what *should* be – the utopias, the ideal republics, the Cloud Cuckoo Lands – looked **actual politics** squarely in the face and wrote about what he saw as honestly as he could.

1 Renaissance Florence

A tumultuous age

Niccolò Machiavelli – in terms of both his career and his thought – was the product of a key moment in the history of **Florence** – one of a number of independent city-states that flourished across Italy during the fifteenth century. Although Florence was ostensibly a republic and could boast one of the most democratic and lively political systems in Europe, in reality this prosperous city-state was ruled by a single family – the wealthy, charismatic **Medici**.

Machiavelli's career and thought grew out of a key moment in the history of Florence

Under the Medici, Florence was not only the centre of an **energetic economy**, at the heart of which stood the woollen and banking industries, but also of a vibrant **literary and artistic culture**. Indeed, Florence was the matrix of that brilliant cultural blossoming that today we know as the **Renaissance**.

In this chapter we will look at:

* a timeline of the tumultuous history of Florence during Machiavelli's lifetime
* key members of the Medici family
* the Florentine Republic
* the Florentine Renaissance and humanism.

Timeline

In the 1480s – when Machiavelli was a very young man – Florence was at its dazzling apogee, under the rule of Lorenzo de' Medici. However, by the 1490s the city, together with the rest of Italy, had fallen prey to **foreign invasion** and violent **civil strife**.

1492	Lorenzo de' Medici ('the Magnificent') dies and is succeeded by his son Piero II ('the Unfortunate')
1494	The French king Charles VIII invades northern Italy, and Piero, after a brief resistance, surrenders. The Florentines rebel against Medici rule, Piero II is sent into exile, and the Florentine Republic is restored, largely under the influence of the dogmatic, firebrand monk **Girolamo Savonarola**
1498	Savonarola is deposed and burned at the stake
1509	The **Florentine Republic** flourishes under the leadership of Piero Soderini; Machiavelli serves as **Second Chancellor**
1512	A bloodless revolution restores Medici rule to Florence
1527	Italy is once again over-run by foreign invaders: in Florence, the Medici are deposed and **a new republic** set up, although it is short lived …

● The city-state of Florence at its height in the 1480s

The changing fortunes of the Medici

The Medici rulers – from the successful and popular Lorenzo the Magnificent to the abject failure Piero the Unfortunate – were the prime examples of 'princes' that Machiavelli had before him as he was writing *The Prince*. Here are some pen portraits of these by turns reviled and admired rulers:

Lorenzo de' Medici ('the Magnificent'), 1449–92 Ruled over Florence (1469–92) at the height of its prosperity, helped to maintain a fragile peace in Italy, and a passionate patron of the arts and humanist culture.

Piero II de' Medici ('the Unfortunate'), 1472–1503 Incompetent and arrogant, Piero quickly proved unable to lead Florence at a time of crisis and went into exile in 1494 when full republican rule was returned to the city.

6

Giovanni di Lorenzo de' Medici, 1475–1521 Masterminded attempts to re-impose Medici rule in Florence and achieved this in 1512; in 1413 was elected Pope as Leo X; his system of indulgences to pay for the new St Peter's Basilica in Rome helped unleash the Protestant Reformation.

Giulio di Giuliano de' Medici, 1478–1534 Elected Pope in 1523 as Clement VII and was influential over Florentine politics; commissioned Machiavelli to write *The Florentine Histories*.

Lorenzo II de Piero di Medici, 1492–1519 Ruled Florence from 1513 to his death from the plague in 1519; Machiavelli dedicated *The Prince* to him.

The Florentine Republic

Savonarola

During the early years of the restored Florentine republic in the 1490s, the dominant force was **Girolamo Savonarola** (1452–98), the prior of San Marco. Savonarola …

* was an ardent republican
* wanted to turn Florence into a 'Christian republic'
* preached against the 'luxuries' of wealthy Florentines.

Savonarola's fundamentalist rule deeply divided the city. In 1497 his followers burned thousands of jewels, cosmetics, books and artworks in the Piazza della Signoria, the city's main square – the infamous **Bonfire of the Vanities**. Soon after, the mood of the city swung against him, and in 1498 he was publicly hanged and burned.

For Machiavelli, Savonarola was an example of the **power of the demagogue**.

Soderini

In 1502 the diplomat Piero Soderini (1450–1522) was elected to the new position of **lifetime gonfaloniere de giustizia**, at the head of the Florentine state.

Unlike the Medici, Soderini was devoted first and foremost to Florence and its people, not to a particular family or faction. Under his direction, the republican government was, for the most part, moderate and free of corruption. It was under Soderini that Machiavelli served for much of his civil service career. For Machiavelli, Soderini came to represent the limitations of the **good but essentially spineless leader**. He was effective only so long as the times were good:

'When afterwards there came a time which required him to drop his patience and his humility, he could not bring himself to do it; so that both he and his country were ruined.'

The Florentine Renaissance

Fifteenth-century Florence was the birthplace of the Renaissance. Through the **patronage** of families such as the Medici, the city developed an extraordinarily rich and daringly innovative **culture of art and architecture, thought and literature:**

* the architectural and engineering feats of Filippo Brunelleschi
* the mythological/philosophical paintings of Sandro Botticelli
* the neoplatonic writings of the philosopher Marsilio Ficino.

It was this fertile environment of intellectual enquiry, in which achievement and creativity were vaunted, that helped shape the mind of the young Machiavelli.

10

● The people of the Renaissance strove to emulate the great thinkers and artists of the ancient world

Humanism

At the heart of the Florentine Renaissance was the philosophical and civic movement known as humanism. This complex movement was characterized by:

✴ a turning away from what was considered the rigid, doctrinaire thought of the Middle Ages towards a spirit of **free intellectual enquiry**

✴ a looking back to the writings and thought of the **ancient Greeks and Romans**, especially the philosophical work of Plato

✴ a belief in **human ingenuity**, rather than an absolute trust in God

✴ a firm belief in the value of **education** for the well-being of both the individual and society.

As you read through this book, think about how these ideas can be seen to be reflected in and deepened by Machiavelli's thought.

2 Life

Renaissance 'bad boy'?

Machiavelli has the reputation of being the **'bad boy'** of the Renaissance. Only decades after his death his name had become a byword for everything underhand, devious, even diabolical …

The real Machiavelli was, however, rather different – his numerous extant letters reveal him as thoughtful and grave, a good friend and, for the times, a loyal and loving husband and father. His books – including the notorious *The Prince* – show him to have been a **shrewd observer** of the political world and a startlingly original thinker.

Machiavelli was a shrewd observer and a startlingly original thinker

● Was Machiavelli really so 'Machiavellian'?

In this chapter we will look at Machiavelli's life:

* his career as a **statesman** and diplomat
* his work as a **writer** and **thinker**
* his principal works, and
* how he won his **notoriety** after his death.

Youth and public life

While comparatively little is known about Machiavelli's early life, his adult life – much of which was spent in the public eye – is richly documented.

3 May 1469 Niccolò di Bernardo de Machiavelli is born in Florence, the son of a **down-at-heel gentleman lawyer**; as a boy he is tutored by the humanist scholar Paolo da Ronciglione and is usually thought to have studied at the University of Florence.

1498 Appointed as **Second Chancellor** and **Secretary to the Ten of Liberty and Peace** – overseeing the military and diplomatic affairs of the Republic of Florence.

1500 Goes on a six-month mission to the French court.

1501 Marries Marietta Corsini.

1506 Sets up the first Florentine militia.

Whosoever desires constant success must change his conduct with the times.

Machiavelli, *The Prince*

The diplomat

Machiavelli won himself a reputation as a **shrewd and effective diplomat** in what was the first great age of European diplomacy. Among his missions were delegations to the French king Louis XII, the Holy Roman Emperor Maximilian I and the Pope.

During the Renaissance the cosmopolitan courts of Europe thronged with ambassadors, emissaries and couriers. High-minded, gorgeously phrased letters ricocheted from monarch to monarch, while protracted treaty negotiations were set off by elaborate ceremony. This **golden surface** of diplomacy, however, barely disguised the **seething underbelly** of intrigue, double dealing and downright treachery.

It is this ambiguous, dangerous world that Machiavelli describes so acutely in his most famous work, *The Prince*.

The man of letters

1509 Machiavelli oversees the **reconquest of Pisa** – the high point of his political career.

1512 The Medici return to power and Machiavelli is **dismissed** from the Chancellery.

1513 He is accused of plotting against the Medici and is tried, imprisoned and **tortured**. He is released and retires to his estate at **Sant'Andrea de Percusinna** outside Florence, where he devotes himself to study and writing. He completes **The Prince**, and copies of the manuscript later circulate among the Florentine 'intelligentsia'.

● In 'exile', Machiavelli devoted himself to a life of study and writing

18

In a letter to his friend Francesco Vettori, Machiavelli described his evening *humanist studies* after a hard day's hunting:

'On the coming of evening, I return to my house and enter my study; and at the door I take off the day's clothing, covered with mud and dust, and put on garments regal and courtly; and reclothed appropriately, I enter the ancient courts of ancient men, where, received by them with affection, I feed on that food which only is mine and which I was born for, where I am not ashamed to speak with them and to ask them the reason for their actions; and they in their kindness answer me; and for four hours of time I do not feel boredom, I forget every trouble, I do not dread poverty, I am not frightened by death; entirely I give myself over to them.'

Return to favour

1516 Becomes a member of the elite literary and philosophical discussion group that meets at the **Orti Oricellari** in Florence.

1518 Machiavelli writes his dramatic masterpiece, *The Mandrake*. His slow return to favour with the Medici is signalled by a commission to write **an official history of Florence** from Cardinal Giulio de' Medici (later Pope Clement VII).

Machiavelli's friends

Throughout his adult life two of Machiavelli's closest friends were the important Florentine historian **Francesco Guicciardini** (1483–1540), whose most famous work was a thoroughly documented *History of Italy*, and the Florentine diplomat **Francesco Vettori** (1474–1539). Machiavelli wrote his friends dozens of letters, discussing his work, probing new ideas and asking advice.

1521	Publication of *The Art of War* – the only one of Machiavelli's political works to be published in his lifetime.
1526	He goes to Rome to present *The Florentine Histories* to his Medici patron Pope Clement VIII.
21 June 1527	He dies in Florence and is buried in Santa Croce.

Portraits

Most of the **surviving portraits** of Machiavelli were created in the decades following his death when he and his writings became famous, even notorious. One of the most famous painted portraits was by the Florentine artist *Santi de Tito* (1536–1603), and shows what has become the **iconic image** of the Florentine thinker – soberly dressed, with a penetrating gaze and knowing smile. It is held in the Musei Civici Fiorentini – you can search for it on the Internet.

Reputation

After his death and the official publication of *The Prince* in 1532, Machiavelli's name spread throughout Europe. The **flagrant amoralism** of his treatise tended to colour his whole reputation and the man himself became a kind of anti-icon of the age – shorthand for everything that was **corrupt** about European, and especially Italian and Catholic, politics:

* French Protestant Huguenots blamed his ideas for the duplicity of the Catholic court and the St Bartholomew Day's Massacre.
* In many Renaissance plays, Machiavelli appears almost like a **pantomime villain** – for example, in Christopher Marlow's *Jew of Malta*.
* *The Prince* influenced Shakespeare's characterization of his anti-heroes, such as **Richard III**, Iago (in *Othello*) and Edmund (in *King Lear*).

Machiavelli – shorthand for everything that was corrupt about European, and especially Italian and Catholic, politics

Principal works

Most of Machiavelli's political writings were circulated as manuscripts during his lifetime and published posthumously:

* *Dell'arte della Guerra* (*The Art of War*, 1521) A **treatise on war** in the form of a Socratic dialogue.
* *La Mandragola* (*The Mandrake Root*, 1524(?)) A **play**.
* *Discorsi sopra la Prima Deca di Tito Livio* (*Discourses on the First Ten Books of Titus Livius*, 1531) Ostensibly a long commentary on the Roman historian Livy but in reality **a treatise on republicanism**.
* *Il Principe* (*The Prince*, 1532) A treatise on the qualities of the absolute ruler and **realism** in politics.
* *Istorie Fiorentine* (*The Florentine Histories*, 1532) An **official history of Florence** written for the Medici.

3 Political theory

An eye on the past

Deeply immersed in the humanist culture of the Renaissance, Machiavelli was very familiar with the great works of **political theory and philosophy of the past** – both those of ancient Greece and Rome and of the Christian thinkers of the Middle Ages.

As a consequence, works such as *The Prince* need to be read in the **context** of his giant forebears. Machiavelli writes almost as if he was engaged in a **sustained dialogue** with their works, one eye always on the past, even as he contemplates the present.

For all that – like the artists of the Florentine Renaissance, who also looked back to the ancients in order to create anew – Machiavelli ended up writing works that radically broke with the past. It is not too much to say that he **transformed** the whole field of political philosophy, deflecting its path away from the ideal and towards the here and now.

In this chapter we will look at:

* what political philosophy is
* the political works of Plato and Aristotle
* St Augustine and Machiavelli's contemporary Thomas More
* Machiavelli as the father of modern political theory.

What is political philosophy?

The word **'politics'** derives from the Greek word for 'city' – *polis* – and refers to the business of 'governing a city' (or a country and so on).

Political philosophy and its close sibling **political science** concern themselves with the ideas and values that underpin (or should underpin) politics. They ask two key questions:

1 What are the possible **forms** of political organization (e.g. monarchy, oligarchy, democracy, etc.)?
2 How should we **judge** political organization and by what **values** (e.g. freedom, equality, the well-being of the many or the state)?

● *Monarchy* – the government by one of the many

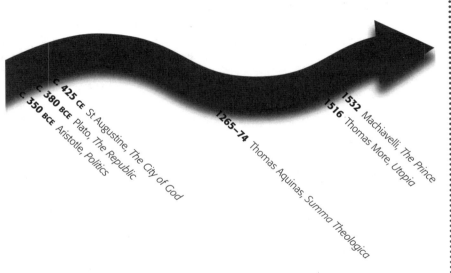

c. **350 BCE** Aristotle, *Politics*

c. **380 BCE** Plato, *The Republic*

c. **425 CE** St Augustine, *The City of God*

1265–74 Thomas Aquinas, *Summa Theologica*

1516 Thomas More, *Utopia*

1532 Machiavelli, *The Prince*

Plato and Aristotle

Two figures loom large over the history of political thought – the ancient Greek philosophers Plato and Aristotle. While he hardly mentions them by name, it is clear that Machiavelli is often wrestling with their heritage in his mind, always countering their **idealism** with his **realism**.

Plato's *Republic*

Plato's great work of political philosophy is *The Republic*, a long dialogue in ten books written in around 380 BCE. In it:

❋ Plato (or rather his mouthpiece, 'Socrates') imagines an **ideal city-state** – the Republic – in which the ultimate goal is justice (e.g. there is male–female equality, no private wealth, etc.).

❋ The city-state is ruled by an impartial and wise **philosopher-king** who acts only for the good of the state.

Although some critics have seen *The Republic* almost as a political manifesto for a real state, most consider it to be an **allegory** or a kind of platform for the elaboration of political ideas.

Aristotle's *Politics*

Plato's great political work has a strong esoteric or mystical flavour. His pupil Aristotle's work, *Politics*, is altogether more **down to earth** and **systematic** but nonetheless is more concerned with **abstract ideas and theories** than with the nitty-gritty of government.

Aristotle conceived of three main types of government, each of which has good and bad forms:

GOOD (works for the common good of the city-state)	Royalty	Aristocracy (government by 'the best')	Constitutional government (government by laws)
BAD (works for the good of only a group)	Tyranny	Oligarchy (government by the wealthy few)	Democracy (anarchy)

There is a strong **ethical quality** in Aristotle's thought – the point of the state is to enable its citizens to **act well**.

Christian political philosophy and beyond

The **idealist bent** of classical political philosophy continued throughout the Christian period, evident in major works at either end of the timespan between the Late Antique period and the Renaissance – *The City of God* by St Augustine of Hippo and *Utopia* by Thomas More.

Augustine's *The City of God*

In his panoramic work *The City of God*, Augustine set out the progress of human history as a struggle between two competing 'orders' – the **City of God** and the **City of Man** – with the inevitable but yet-to-be-realized victory of the former. While the City of God distils the eternal values of Christianity, the City of Man – as notably represented by ancient Rome – represents the ephemeral affairs of mankind.

For St Augustine, the ideal City of Man would reflect, and be subordinate to, the City of God.

32

Thomas More's *Utopia*

In *Utopia*, written roughly at the same time as *The Prince*, the English lawyer set out a **fantastic vision** of an ideal society named Utopia (from the Greek for 'no place'), somewhere in the New World. Its features included:

* no private wealth
* a welfare state, including free medical care
* religious tolerance
* a 6-hour working day.

Part of More's intention was to satirize his own society, but it seems probable that he was also setting out a 'real' (though admittedly pie-in-the-sky) political programme for the ideal city-state.

● More's *Utopia* included a short working day – dream on!

The Machiavellian revolution

Unmentioned, Aristotle and Plato nonetheless lurk in the shadows of Machiavelli's *The Prince*:

'Many have imagined republics and principalities which have never been seen or known to exist in reality; for how we live is so far removed from how we ought to live, that he who abandons what is done for what ought to be done, will rather bring about his ruin rather than his salvation.'

In this short, caustic passage from *The Prince*, Machiavelli **topples the utopian project** of his great predecessors in political philosophy. Such 'dreams' are simply futile, even destructive, he warns; he has another objective – **'to go straight to the truth of things'**.

Machiavelli …

* accepts (even as he abhors) **human nature** as it is – which, as he sees it, is motivated by self-interest and the lust for power (none of Aristotle's virtuous citizens here, all desperate to act well)
* seeks to show how a city-state might keep these base motivations **in check** and even **harness** them for the stability and prosperity of the whole
* seeks to give **useful, pragmatic advice** to rulers.

Means and ends

The revolution represented in political thought by Machiavelli is often summed up in the proverbial 'The ends justify the means.' Throughout *The Prince*, Machiavelli represents his ruler undertaking acts that, while morally objectionable in themselves, nonetheless have good outcomes. For example, the merciless punishment of a rebel can be justified in that it promotes stability and peace by quelling further rebellion.

4 The Prince I

Dirty hands

What makes a good political leader?

1 A virtuous life and a **principled stance** when faced with difficult decisions? – *or* –
2 A strong-minded, even ruthless, approach that, as much out of self-interest as the interests of the state, sacrifices ethical high-mindedness to **expediency**?

In his short treatise *The Prince*, Machiavelli daringly opted for the latter. His message was **shocking** and **revolutionary**: if a ruler – and the state he rules – is to survive and flourish:

He must be prepared to ditch conventional morality and get his hands dirty

The concept of a 'Prince'

It is important to remember that when Machiavelli refers to a prince, he does not necessarily mean a 'royal ruler', but uses the term more broadly to mean any political leader – whether a tyrant who has seized power by force, an aristocrat who has inherited his position or an elected citizen.

In this chapter we will look at:

* the personal and literary context in which *The Prince* was written
* Machiavelli's worldview, as presented in *The Prince*
* his understanding of human nature
* the qualities of Machiavelli's 'Prince'.

How things are ... not should be

Machiavelli would eventually dedicate *The Prince* to one of the Medici, the powerful Florentine family who, in 1512, had seized back power. The book was thus an attempt to curry favour with the new regime. Although he was not above flattery, in *The Prince* Machiavelli set out to examine the political world with a **clear, objective eye**:

> **Since it is my intention to write something useful to those of understanding, it seems best to me to go straight to the actual truth of things rather than to dwell in dreams.**
>
> *The Prince, XV*

Machiavelli was not the slightest bit interested in creating a utopian (idealized) vision of a ruler and his state. His concern was to present human nature as he considered it really to be.

The Mirror of Princes

The Prince was part of a medieval and Renaissance literary tradition known as the 'Mirror of Princes'. This was a political treatise dedicated to a king or prince in which thinkers set out a flattering portrait of the ideal Christian ruler. In 1516, for example, the Dutch humanist scholar Erasmus wrote *Institutio principis Christiani* (*The Education of a Christian Prince*), which he dedicated to Charles I of Spain.

Machiavelli's and Erasmus's works could hardly be more different: while *The Education* was an erudite essay in Latin about the virtuous ruler's role as the earthly representative of God, *The Prince* was a robust, pithy and frankly amoral guide in everyday Italian to the cut and thrust of political life.

The nature of the world: providence or fortune?

The traditional view

The conventional medieval and Renaissance worldview was that, however superficially chaotic life might appear to be, it is ultimately governed by a **rational order** designed by God. This was the Christian doctrine of **providence**, by which all that happens in the world is the unfolding of a divinely ordained plan. Ultimately, the good will be rewarded and the evil punished.

Machiavelli's view

Machiavelli dismissed this view out of hand. For him, the world was unpredictable, precarious and in **constant flux**, ruled over by chance.

● For Machiavelli, human affairs were, to a degree, a matter of sheer luck

'... all human affairs are in a state of flux.'

Fortuna
Machiavelli used the ancient Roman goddess Fortuna as a personification of the vagaries of 'human affairs' – an 'unstable and fickle deity' who 'turns states and kingdoms upside down as she pleases' and 'deprives the just of the good that she freely gives to the unjust'.

Despite what might be argued to be a pessimistic viewpoint, Machiavelli insisted …

* that people should not passively accept the ups and downs of fortune, *but*
* that they should attempt to turn events to their advantage at every turn.

'I believe that even if it is true that fortune governs half our lives, she still allows us to take control of the other half …'

Human nature

In his famous chapter on 'cruelty and mercy' (see Chapter 5), Machiavelli gives us a bleak and distinctly unsentimental view of human nature:

'For one can generally say this about men: they are ungrateful, fickle, simulators and deceivers, avoiders of danger, and greedy for grain ...'

For Machiavelli, humans beings:

* are motivated by self-interest
* act more out of a fear of punishment than a desire to do what is right
* are untrustworthy and disloyal.

In this respect, Machiavelli is to a large degree in accord with ...

* traditional Christian thought (e.g. St Augustine), for whom human nature was 'fallen' (i.e. innately corrupt)
* contemporary Renaissance observers, who wrote in the context of an early sixteenth-century Europe that was wracked by war, revolt and schism.

Machiavelli was unusual, however, in using human fallibility as the **foundation for a political philosophy**: the successful ruler must have a clear-eyed view of how his subjects are likely to act and be prepared to exploit their weaknesses.

It is a point of view that looks forward to the thought of the English political philosopher Thomas Hobbes, for whom the natural condition of mankind (were there no political community) is a **'war of all against all'** – amoral anarchy.

Machiavelli [has] a bleak and distinctly unsentimental view of human nature ...

What is a 'good' prince?

The traditional view

From classical times onwards the ideal ruler was also a morally virtuous one, a shepherd of his people and a representative of God on earth:

> We take it for granted that a good ruler is both good and wise ...

Aristotle

> The worthy exercise of the kingly office ... requires ... excelling virtue and must be requited by a high degree of blessedness.

St Thomas Aquinas

> ... a celestial creature .... more like a divine being than a mortal, yea, sent by God above to help the affairs of mortals by looking out and caring for everyone and everything ... who works and strives night and day for just one end – to be the best he can for everyone.

Erasmus

Machiavelli's view

Machiavelli was scornful of such idealistic notions, which he believed had very little to do with reality. For him, the 'good' prince was someone who …

✳ uses his wits and acts courageously
✳ acts ruthlessly *where necessary*
✳ is ready to 'act in harmony with the times', changing his game plan to match changing circumstances.

Virtù

For Machiavelli, the most important virtue of the good prince was *virtù*. This has little to do with the English term 'virtue', but roughly equates with 'manliness' (*vir* is the Latin word for 'man') and suggests the associated conventional qualities of men – courage, forcefulness, determination and so on. It was *virtù* that enabled a man to rise to power and stay there.

5 The Prince II

What makes a good ruler?

The Prince takes the form of 26 short, spare chapters, each of which deals with an aspect of political rule. Here are some typical chapter titles:

* VIII Of those who become princes through wickedness
* XII A prince's duty concerning military matters
* XVI Of generosity and miserliness
* XXIII Of how to avoid flatterers

Machiavelli wrote in an economical but elegant Italian, not Latin (thereby making it accessible beyond an educated elite), and peppered his prose with pointed epigrams (witty 'sound bites', examples of which you will find throughout this book).

In this chapter, we will look at:

* the different ways in which a ruler can rise to power
* how a ruler should use fear and cunning
* how we should interpret *The Prince* – at face value or as satire?

The rise to power

In Chapters VI, VII and VII of *The Prince* Machiavelli explores how rulers gain power in a state.

1 The ruler comes to power by dint of his own force of will (*virtù*)

For example, by conquering a city with his troops. As exempla of such princes Machiavelli cites a mixture of classical, mythical and biblical heroes – Cyrus, Theseus, Romulus and Moses.

A ruler who comes to power this way will more easily remain secure in that power, as he has already won the respect of his new subjects.

2 The ruler comes to power by fortune

For example, he is granted a state because he is rich or enjoys the favour of another, more powerful ruler. According to Machiavelli, this ruler is more likely to find it difficult to keep power because he has not yet proved his *virtù*.

3 The ruler comes to power by criminal *virtù*

For example, by murdering the previous ruler. Machiavelli, it comes as a relief to read, disapproves of this method!

4 The ruler is elected to power by his fellow citizens

(See Chapter 6.)

Of cruelty and mercy

Chapter VII of *The Prince*, 'Of cruelty and mercy', is one of the most famous in the book and concerns a central dilemma of the ruler:

'... whether it is better to be loved than to be feared, or the contrary ...'

Machiavelli is asking:

* Should the prince keep power over the ruled by **sheer terror** – e.g. by acts of cruelty? – *or* –
* Should he try to win their loyalty by making himself **loved** – e.g. by being merciful.

● Should the Prince rule by fear … or by love?

Machiavelli **flies in the face** of the Christian ideal of the Prince – in whom the capacity for mercy was essential. Machiavelli justifies his stance in the following way:

> ### 'Since men love at their own pleasure and fear at the pleasure of the prince, the wise prince should build that which is his own, not upon that which belongs to others.'

55

What Machiavelli means here is that a ruler cannot depend on his subjects' love – which can be taken away at any moment – but he *can* depend on his own ability to keep control.

However, as ever, he tempers this harsh 'truth', by adding that the ruler must act brutally only **with good reason** – to keep order and keep his subjects 'united and loyal'. Otherwise he risks earning his subjects' **hatred**.

Cunning

From the sixteenth century onwards, popular use of the term 'Machiavellian' was used to refer to anything cunning, nefarious or underhand. **Cunning, treachery** and **deceit** are the subjects of another key chapter, XVIII – the ironically titled 'How a prince should keep his word'. Only when it suits him, comes the inevitable answer.

Again, Machiavelli draws on experience:

56

'One sees from experience in our times that the princes who have accomplished great deeds are those who have thought little about keeping faith and who have known how cunningly to manipulate men's minds.'

Machiavelli goes on to give a defence of treachery and hypocrisy – incidentally providing one of the most shocking passages in the whole of *The Prince*:

> *But since men are a wicked lot and will not keep their promises to you, you likewise need not keep yours to them. A prince never lacks legitimate reasons to colour over his failure to keep his word […] But it is necessary to know how to colour over this nature effectively, and to be a great pretender and dissembler. He who deceives will always find someone who will let himself be deceived.*

Pope Alexander VI

Machiavelli's exemplum here is the Renaissance Pope Alexander VI (reigned 1492–1503), better known under his name Rodrigo Borgia and notorious, even in his times, for his brutality and double dealing (as well as his string of mistresses). According to Machiavelli, he 'never did anything else, nor thought about anything else than to deceive men'.

Renaissance manual or republican satire?

How should we read *The Prince*? Or perhaps better: how did Machiavelli's Renaissance readers read *The Prince*?

* Is it a straightforward **self-help guide for Italian princes**, packed with shrewd advice … even an **apology for tyranny**?
* Is it a **bitter republican satire**, an angry attack on the corruption and duplicity of Renaissance rulers who had wreaked so much havoc on his beloved city of Florence?

Both readings are possible and not even mutually exclusive:

* For his Medici masters it might have been read as a flattering portrait of their *virtù* – hadn't Cardinal Giovanni de' Medici fought to win back Florence by might of arms in 1512?
* For a select few, the republican diehards who read *The Prince* when it circulated in Florence in manuscript, it might have been read as a covert cry for a return to republican rule.

Another reading is possible and is the one I personally hold to – that Machiavelli was absolutely sincere in what he wrote (even if he sometimes over-eggs the pudding). He was writing at a terrifying time in Italian history, and he knew that what Florence, and indeed the whole of Italy, needed, above all, was **strong government** – whether monarchical *or* republican.

A self-help guide for Italian princes, a bitter republican satire or simply a call for strong government?

6 The Discourses

Magnum opus

The *Discourses on the First Ten Books of Titus Livius* is a much longer, and more carefully wrought, work than *The Prince*, and Machiavelli clearly considered it his **magnum opus**. Ostensibly a humanist commentary on the multivolume history of ancient Rome written by Titus Livius (59 BCE to 17 CE), it is also a penetrating investigation into republican government.

Which was the 'true' Machiavelli? The seeming apologist for absolute rulers suggested by *The Prince* or the ardent republican of *The Discourses on Livy*? This seeming paradox that an author could have written both books has puzzled readers and commentators ever since.

Which was the 'true' Machiavelli?

Machiavelli started writing *The Discourses* at about the same time as he wrote *The Prince*, in 1513, and did not finish it until around 1517. It was dedicated not to a prince but to two of his friends at the Orti Oricellari. Like *The Prince*, although it remained unpublished until after his death, it circulated in manuscript form during his lifetime.

In this chapter we will look at:

* the Roman republic as Machiavelli's ideal state
* why Machiavelli thought the republic was the best form of government
* how we might reconcile the writer of *The Prince* with the writer of *The Discourses*.

Looking back to Rome

During the Renaissance, thinkers, philosophers and artists all looked back to the ancient Greek world as a **golden age** in human history, when mankind's achievements reached a creative peak that had remained unsurpassed ever since. They sought not only to recover classical literature and art for the modern age but also to emulate, even outdo, them in their own works.

Machiavelli was thoroughly immersed in this **humanist** culture, but was in a sense even more ambitious; he held up the **political achievements** and **values** of the ancients as a model for the contemporary world. Above all, he looked to the ancient Roman Republic as his ideal.

● Machiavelli looked back with nostalgia to the golden age of the classical world and asked 'How did we go wrong?'

64

The Roman Republic

The ancient Roman Republic lasted from 508 to 44 BCE. During this period, Rome was ruled by a tripartite system featuring:

1 the **citizens** – the various assemblies of the male patricians (aristocrats) and plebeians (people)
2 **two consuls** elected annually by the citizens to be the heads of government
3 an appointed **Senate**, which advised the consuls
4 a powerful, if unwritten, **constitution**.

Machiavelli admired the Roman Republic because:

✳ It was remarkably **stable** and **long-lived**.
✳ It had strong **'masculine' values** – courage, honour, determination, etc. – in short, he admired the *virtù* of its leaders, soldiers and citizens.
✳ It represented the possibility of a **unified, peaceful Italy**.

The trouble with the modern age

Christianity

Why, Machiavelli wondered, was modern Italy so disunified and unstable, and so prone to violence, upheaval, invasion and war? Part of the reason, he argued, lay in the Christian religion.

Machiavelli is saying: while Christian values might be good *in themselves*, they did not have a good result, and were maybe even disastrous, politically.

'Our religion has glorified the humble and contemplative man, rather than men of action. It has assigned as man's highest good humility, abnegation and contempt for mundane things, whereas [the religion of the past] identified it with magnanimity, bodily strength, and everything else that makes men bold. And, if our religion demands that in you there be strength, what it asks for is strength to suffer rather than strength to do bold things.'

The church

Machiavelli was even more scathing about the baleful influence of the church in modern Italy. In Renaissance times, the Catholic Church, headed by the Pope, was not only a **religious power** but also a **political/secular** one, ruling a large group of territories in Italy known as the Papal States.

The church, Machiavelli argued, was neither strong enough to exert its control over all Italy nor weak enough to be conquered by another state. Moreover, because of its corruption and immorality, it set a **bad example** to the rest of Italy.

Because of this, Italy was prevented from becoming a powerful, stable principality, as Renaissance France or England had become.

> **'It is the Church that has kept, and keeps, Italy divided.'**

The advantages of republicanism

Machiavelli's admiration for the Roman Republic was not simply the result of nostalgia for the classical world or of some democratic impulse; for him, the republic had **inherent advantages** over other forms of government. These might be summed up as:

1 diversity   2 community   3 synergy.

Diversity

* The key to good government, Machiavelli believed, was an ability to **change with the times**.
* The principality depends on a single man, who often becomes fixed in his ways, and therefore is less able to respond flexibly to a crisis.
* The republic, by contrast, is based upon the abilities of many men and is therefore more **open to change**.

'Government by the populace is better than government by princes.'

Community

* States become great, Machiavelli argued, not because of the well-being of particular individuals, but because of the well-being of the **whole community**.
* The democratic foundation of the republic ensures that it is the happiness of the greatest number rather than the few that is paramount.

Synergy

* Republics call upon, as in ancient Rome, the participation of two main classes – the aristocrats and the ordinary citizens.
* While the interests of these two classes are often at loggerheads, together they produce a kind of **creative tension** that energizes the state and helps keep it prosperous.

● The synergy of the republic …

The real Machiavelli?

During his lifetime, Machiavelli was riven *between*:

* his **republican** sympathies *and*
* the necessity of **going with the times** and of making a living.

This tension is, to an extent, evident in his works:

* In writing *The Prince*, he was practising what he preached – be adaptable and fluid, don't get stuck in your ways. Here was a book that literally courted the times (personified in the Medici).
* In writing *The Discourses*, he was allowing himself more freedom, giving vent to his enthusiasm for the Roman ideal and examining how republics like Florence could actually work without recourse to 'strongman rule'.

Machiavelli was profoundly *of* his time and was prepared to face up to the contradictions and paradoxes that that condition imposed upon him

70

In a sense, it is futile wondering which of these is the **'real' Machiavelli**. Both *The Prince* and *The Discourses* are aspects of the same man – a man who was profoundly *of* his time and who was prepared to face up to the **contradictions** and **paradoxes** that that condition imposed upon him.

Strong government

The Prince and *The Discourses*, of course, are reconcilable in another way – in their over-riding concern for **strong government**. In his lifetime, Machiavelli had repeatedly witnessed the devastating costs of weak rule – be it under a 'monarchy' or republic – and recognized the desperate need for a unified, decisive government in the face of crises such as foreign invasion or internal dissent. While he looked to republicanism as the most effective solution in the long run to state power, in an emergency – when people's prosperity and even their lives were at stake – rule by a strong prince was to be welcomed.

7 Machiavelli and war

The chief business of the state

Throughout his adult life Machiavelli saw the ravages inflicted by war – the trauma of **the French invasion** of Italy in 1494 and the triumph of the Florentine **reconquest of Pisa** in 1509, alike, instilled in him the belief that the success of a state of whatever kind lay in its ability to conduct war.

The political role of war looms large in his writings:

* in three key chapters in *The Prince*
* throughout *The Discourses*
* and in a work devoted to the subject, *The Art of War.*

The political role of war looms large in Machiavelli's writings

In this chapter we will look at:

* Machiavelli's creation of a Florentine militia and his role in the reconquest of Pisa
* his discussion of war in *The Prince*
* his 'Socratic dialogue', *The Art of War*.

● Machiavelli's reflections on war in *The Prince* and elsewhere were rooted in actual experience – both as defeated and conquered victim and triumphant victor

The Florentine militia

Machiavelli's greatest success as a civil servant during the Republic was **the creation of a Florentine militia** in 1506:

* For some two centuries Florence, like most other Italian city-states, had depended on **mercenaries** (hired, foreign professional soldiers) in order to defend itself and to wage war.
* Machiavelli passionately believed that his native city's (and, indeed, Italy's) vulnerability to foreign invasion was due to its lack of a strong **home-grown citizen army**.
* Whereas the mercenaries could be depended on only as long as they were not offered better terms elsewhere, citizens, Machiavelli reasoned, would fight out of loyalty and patriotism.

Italy's ruin can be traced to other cause than her reliance, for so many years, on mercenary armies.

The Prince

In his determination to set up a Florentine militia, Machiavelli, however, was faced with two major hurdles:

1 The ordinary people themselves did not see military service as part of their **duty to the state**.
2 The rich merchants believed that if the workers were armed they would **rise up** against their masters.

Eventually Machiavelli reached a **compromise**: the new militiamen would be drawn, not from the city's workers, but from the **peasants** in its surrounding territory.

Florentine pride

Despite early resistance, the new militia proved successful and popular. One Florentine observer records the citizens' excitement when the first recruits were assembled in the Piazza della Signoria and were given their new uniforms: 'a white waistcoat, a pair of stockings half red and half white, a white cap, shoes and an iron breastplate … '

The reconquest of Pisa

The greatest triumph of the new militia was the key role it played in the reconquest of Pisa.

Florence had first captured this **prosperous port city** more than a hundred years before. During the French invasion of 1494, however, Pisa had seized the opportunity to declare its independence. The loss of Pisa was a grave blow to **Florentine pride** and during the following years the Florentine Republic laboured long and hard to bring the city once again to heel.

Machiavelli the tactician

Although Machiavelli was no solider, as the civil servant in charge of the militia he had a great deal to do with its day-to-day running and even with **military tactics**. He spent much of his time up at the front lines and was closely involved with the negotiations when the Pisans were forced to surrender.

The recovery of Pisa marked the **high point of Machiavelli's political career**. One of his associates fêted him thus: 'May a thousand good fortunes result to you from the great fain of this noble city, for truly you have personally had a great share in the matter … Each day I discover in you a greater prophet than … any generation possessed.'

● With the reconquest of Pisa, Machiavelli stood at the height of his career. His own subsequent fall and 'exile' with the return of the Medici must have helped give grist to his ideas about the vicissitudes of 'fortune'

Of *The Prince* and war

Machiavelli's key arguments about war in *The Prince* are as follows:

Chapter XII

* The survival of a state depends on a good army.
* Mercenary soldiers are 'disunited, ambitious, undisciplined and disloyal' and make the state more vulnerable to reversals of fortune.

Exemplum

On mercenaries, Machiavelli cites the case of the **Venetians**, who had depended on mercenary troops for the conquest of their mainland territories in northern Italy. However, at the **Battle of Vaila** (Agnadello) in 1509, the Venetians were soundly beaten by the French and suddenly 'lost what had cost them 800 years of exhausting effort to acquire'.

Chapter XIII

✻ For much the same reasons, dependence on an ally's troops can be just as disastrous.

Exemplum

Here Machiavelli cites the biblical example of **David**, who, when facing Goliath, preferred to fight with his own simple weapons rather than more sophisticated ones borrowed from his king, Saul. Self-reliance is the key to strength. David, incidentally, was the 'secular saint' of the Florentine Republic: his statue by Michelangelo symbolizes Florentine independence.

Chapter XIV

Machiavelli here attacks the preoccupation of Renaissance rulers with the patronage of the visual arts, sometimes to the detriment of matters of state. The ability to wage war, he concludes, is the foundation on which the whole state rests.

The Art of War

* *The Art of War*, written in around 1519–20 and published in 1521, was **the only political book published in Machiavelli's lifetime**, which may suggest the importance it had for him.
* It takes the form of a **dialogue** largely between Cosimo Rucellai and the fictional 'Fabrizio Colonna', who seems to be a **mouthpiece** for, or even a self-portrait of, Machiavelli.
* The dialogue takes place in the **Orti Oricellari**, the meeting place for Florentine humanists.
* The key theme is, again, the importance of creating a **citizen-based militia**.

'Never lead your soldiers to battle if you have not first confirmed their spirit and known them to be without fear and ordered; and never test them except when you see that they hope to win.'

A critique of Machiavelli as military thinker

Machiavelli's insistence on the central role of a home-grown militia has often drawn criticism as being naive and out of touch – even as the obsession of an armchair tactician preoccupied with the history and practices of **ancient Rome**. In Renaissance Italy, critics point out, ill-equipped citizen-soldiers were a poor match for professional mercenaries – as suggested by the ignominious defeat of the Florentine Republic at Prato in 1512.

However, as we have seen, Machiavelli had **hands-on** experience of warfare (even if only as an administrator and not as a soldier). Moreover, in later times the notion of a standing army drawn from a state's citizenry would became the **established norm** in European warfare.

8 A Machiavellian glossary

The matter of rhetoric

In his writing, Machiavelli uses key terms repeatedly in order to drive home his ideas

Machiavelli is always careful and concise in his use of language. Throughout *The Prince* and *The Discourses* he uses some terms **repeatedly**, thereby reinforcing the structure of his book and driving home his ideas. **Key terms** in his political thought include:

* fortune
* opportunity
* the state
* *virtù*.

Translators often use different English words for a single Italian term, so that sometimes this verbal structure can be weakened or lost.

Rhetoric

In the dedicatory letter that begins *The Prince*, Machiavelli claims that the work is written in a simple and direct way: 'I have not adorned this work nor filled it with long periodic sentences or pompous and magnificent words or any of the other elegant niceties and superficial ornaments with which many writers like to adorn and elaborate their matter … ' Nonetheless, Machiavelli was a master of **rhetoric** – which, in the Renaissance, meant the use of language to **persuade** the listener or reader. Fittingly for a work about the duplicity of power, his simplicity of style masks a desire to convince the reader of his point of view. Do you think that Machiavelli succeeds?

In this chapter we will look at the key terms in Machiavelli's writing, in the form of an A–Z glossary.

Fortune and empire

Fortune – *Fortuna*

Throughout his writings Machiavelli often personified fortune as a capricious woman or as the ancient Roman goddess Fortuna, 'who turns states and kingdoms upside down as she pleases'. Fortune, for Machiavelli, is sometimes not only a question of mere chance, but a kind of **wanton havoc**. On the other hand, fortune sometimes throws out an **opportunity** to those who are alert:

88

> **And since Fortune wants to do everything, she wishes us to let her do it, to be quiet, and not to give her trouble, and to wait for a time when she will allow something to be done by men.**
>
> Letter to Vettori, 1513

The ruler who has *virtù* knows how to rise above Fortune and seize the opportunities she, from time to time, throws out.

Bullet Guide: Machiavelli

Machiavelli personifies fortune as a woman – in the Renaissance stereotyped as capricious and undependable but sometimes capable of being tamed

Empire – *imperio*

Machiavelli, like many Renaissance thinkers, looked back on the Roman Empire with awe and admiration, as a time when the rule of law and justice united a vast number of territories and peoples. However, he distinguished between 'good' and 'bad' empires:

✗ *an empire based upon the **dominion** of one people over another*
✔ *an empire based on the **voluntary association** and collaboration of peoples.*

The former was inherently flawed and unstable, whereas the latter led to prosperity and peace.

Liberty and opportunity

Liberty – *libertà*

For Machiavelli, liberty is an ultimate value that found its best expression in the **republican** form of government, whereby citizens, he thought, are more likely to defend their freedom from oppression. In a monarchy or oligarchy, by contrast, the conception of freedom is narrowed to mean the freedom of the few to control the majority, and the larger sense of liberty is exchanged for mere **security**.

'Where the very safety of the country depends upon the resolution to be taken, no consideration of justice or injustice, humanity or cruelty, nor of glory or of shame, should be allowed to prevail. But putting all other considerations aside, the only question should be: What course will save the life and liberty of the country?'

Opportunity – *occasione*

The ruler with *virtù* makes good use of every opportunity that **fortune** throws up. It was an important idea for Machiavelli who may have seen the years of the Florentine Republic as a lost opportunity both for himself and for the city. He even wrote a poem in which opportunity is personified (like fortune) as female:

> **And you who stand here talking, you who dote**
> **On idle chatter, while the hour lingers,**
> **Wise up a bit, you idiot, you've missed the boat,**
> **And I've already slipped between your fingers!**

'On Occasion', lines 19–22

At the end of *The Prince*, Machiavelli casts the prostration of Italy owing to war and invasion as the supreme opportunity for a saviour-prince to express his *virtù*.

Order and security

Order – *ordoni*

Political 'order' is a crucial concept for Machiavelli, and the word recurs with almost obsessive frequency across his writings. Order is often contrasted with the disorder sown by fortune and must be the **primary goal** of good government. Order leads to peace and prosperity.

Security – *securità*

In Machiavelli's thought, he often sets the political goal of **security** against that of **liberty**. A state that wishes to maintain internal stability and unity is often tempted to do so by making its people weak – that is, by **disarming them**. This security is bought at the cost of liberty and ultimately of the long-term viability of the state.

Exemplum

In *The Discourses* Machiavelli points to France as an example of a state in which security has become almost the be-all and end-all of politics. In so doing, however, France has sown the seeds of its own destruction, since its king is ultimately dependent on foreign mercenaries:

'This all comes from having disarmed his people and having preferred […] to enjoy the immediate profit of being able to plunder the people and of avoiding an imaginary rather than a real danger, instead of doing things that would assure them and make their states perpetually happy. This disorder, if it produces some quiet times, is in time the cause of straitened circumstances, damage and irreparable ruin.'

State to *virtù*

The state – *stato*

Machiavelli uses the word *stato* frequently in *The Prince* but what exactly he means by the term has been much debated:

❉ Some critics argue that he uses *stato* in what was in the Renaissance its conventional sense – to mean simply the **dominion possessed by a prince**.

❉ Others insist that Machiavelli is grappling towards the modern meaning of the term – that is, the notion of an **impersonal political institution** that holds a monopoly of power over a defined territory.

Virtù

For Machiavelli, *virtù* has nothing to do with 'virtue', in its Christian sense of a morally good quality, such as patience or charity, but is the **essential quality of the effective ruler**. It can comprise everything from ingenuity and cunning to virility and warlike prowess and is always characterized as **masculine** and **active**. In *The Prince* active, 'male' *virtù* is again and again contrasted with 'feminine' fortune – the raw material that the ruler must mould to his will.

The will to power

Machiavellian *virtù* often seems to foreshadow the concept of the 'will to power' as conceived by the nineteenth-century German philosopher Friedrich Nietzsche – the ruthless desire to dominate and control. Machiavelli's Prince, in his jettisoning of conventional morality, disregard for Christian 'weakness' and display of virile strength, might be argued to prefigure Nietzsche's *Übermensch*, or 'Super-person'.

●Machiavelli's *virtù* is above all an active, masculine energy – the ambition to dominate and control

9 Machiavelli: Renaissance man

Playwright, poet, historian ...

During the enforced retirement of his later years, Machiavelli turned his hand to **many kinds of writing** – to win the patronage of the Medici, to earn himself badly needed money and, last but not least, to keep himself intellectually alert and engaged. Among his writings are:

* **political treatises** such as *The Prince*
* **historical studies** such as *The Florentine Histories*
* **poetry and plays** (notably *The Mandrake*) ...

Machiavelli's career as a writer enabled him to re-engage with the Florentine elite – both socially and intellectually – and principally through the gatherings that took place in the **Orti Oricellari** gardens.

Machiavelli's career as a writer enabled him to re-engage with the Florentine elite – both socially and intellectually ...

● ●

In this chapter we will look at:

✴ Machiavelli's association with the Orti Oricellari
✴ his success as a playwright
✴ *The Florentine Histories*
✴ his private letters as a record of his life and ideas.

The Orti Oricellari

In 1516 Machiavelli began to frequent the **informal intellectual gatherings** held at the Orti Oricellari – a beautiful, tranquil garden owned by the wealthy Rucellai family in the heart of Florence. By now Machiavelli was already famous (among the Florentine elite at least) as the author of *The Prince*, which, although as yet unpublished, was already attracting attention for its trenchant arguments and razor wit.

The Orti Oricellari was the heir to the celebrated **Platonic Academy**, which had flourished during the time of Lorenzo the Magnificent as a springboard for the city's humanist culture. For Machiavelli, his admission to these elite gatherings enabled him to re-establish himself at the heart of Florentine society.

● The refined atmosphere of the Orti Oricellari gardens provides a backdrop to the intellectual pursuits and writings of Machiavelli's last decade

Other frequenters of the Orti Oricellari

❋ **Francesco Guicciardini** A statesman and important historian whose most famous work is *History of Italy* (1537–40).

❋ **Cosimo Rucellai** The aristocratic and kindly patron of the gatherings, grandson of the founder of the Orti Oricellari, Bernardo Rucellai.

❋ **Anton-Francesco degli Albizzi** A member of a family that had in earlier times been a rival to the Medici family; a dedicatee of *The Discourses*.

❋ **Zanobi Buondelmonti** Another dedicatee of *The Discourses*.

In *The Art of War*, Machiavelli evokes the gatherings at the Orti Oricellari: '… since the days were long and the weather intensely hot, Cosimo [Rucellai] […] took his guests to the most retired and shady part of the gardens. […] Fabrizio [i.e. Machiavelli's mouthpiece] said it was a most delightful garden.'

The playwright

Ironically, it was as a playwright that Machiavelli received most acclaim during his lifetime. At this time Italian theatre was somewhat crude and undeveloped, and once again Machiavelli turned to the classical world – and especially to the **Latin comedies of Plautus** (254–184 BCE) – for his inspiration.

Machiavelli's best play is *La Mandragola* (*The Mandrake Root*), which was completed in 1518 and first performed before his friends at the Orti Oricellari. In this rumbustious but erudite farce, a young aristocrat, Callimaco, is in love with a beautiful young married woman, Lucretia, and convinces her much older husband that he will only have a son and heir if he gives his wife a fertility drug made from the root of the mandrake (a plant famed for its associations with witchcraft) …

As the drug, Callimaco lies, will be lethal to the first man who has sex with Lucretia, he suggests to the husband that he has to find some dupe to take his place in the marriage bed. Callimaco, in disguise, plays the dupe, fools the husband and ends up getting the beautiful, young wife.

It might be expected that a serious thinker like Machiavelli, with such a bleak worldview, would have written tragedies not comedies. However, the cynical notion that conventional virtue is pretty worthless in a corrupt world, and that **duplicity is more often rewarded than punished**, is common to both *The Mandrake Root* and *The Prince*.

Surprisingly – given its satiric portrayal of sexual morality and the church – *The Mandrake Root* was warmly applauded by the Pope when it was later performed at the Vatican. The play is still revered as a classic of Italian – indeed, world – theatre.

The historian

* By the 1520s Machiavelli was still eager to win the favour of the Medici family, and in 1521 he accepted a commission from Cardinal Giulio de' Medici (1478–1534; Pope Clement VII from 1523) to write a history of Florence.
* He was paid 100 *fiorini de studio* per year for 2 years to finish the work – a not especially generous sum.
* He finally presented the work to Pope Clement in 1526.
* *The Florentine Histories* is Machiavelli's longest, but possibly also least-read, book.

The Florentine Histories is Machiavelli's longest, but possibly also least-read, book

104

Through the eight volumes of *The Florentine Histories*, Machiavelli traced the development of the Florentine Republic since medieval times, emphasizing the role played by the **internal strife** between the various factions. He compares the destructive effects of the infighting in Florence to its constructive role in ancient Rome:

[The struggles] in Rome ended in law, those in Florence with the exile and death of many citizens; those in Rome always increased military virtue, those in Florence eliminated it altogether.

In this way, Machiavelli was able to **flatter the Medici family** by showing them as having brought order to Florence, even as they tore apart its republican institutions. Judiciously, he also chose to end his history with the death of Florence's greatest ruler, Lorenzo the Magnificent, in 1492.

The letter writer

Miraculously, a large number of Machiavelli's **private letters** to his friends (as well as letters *to* him) have survived and provide a fascinating and sometimes moving insight into the **life** and **evolving ideas** of the Renaissance thinker. Many of the letters were addressed to his friend, the Florentine diplomat Francesco Vettori (1474–1539). Here are a few sample passages:

To his son Guido:

> *I have never so longed to return to Florence as I do now ... Simply tell her [Machiavelli's wife, Marietta] that, whatever she hears, she should be of good cheer, since I shall be there before any danger comes. Kiss Baccina, Piero and Totto [...] Live in happiness and spend as little as you can ...*

To Vettori, in 1513, of his reading of the Greek and Roman classics:

> *I enter into the courts filled with ancient men where, affectionately received, I nourish myself on that food that alone is mine and for which I was born; where I am unashamed to converse and ask them to explain their actions, and where they, kindly, answer me. And for four hours at a time I feel no boredom, I forget all my troubles, I have no fear of poverty or even death.*

To Vettori, in 1513, after his release from prison:

> *I should like you to get this pleasure from these troubles of mine, that I have borne them so straightforwardly that I am proud of myself for it and consider myself more of a man than I believed I was.*

Machiavelli's private letters ... provide a fascinating and sometimes moving insight into the life and evolving ideas of the Renaissance thinker

10 Influence

Man of parts

Machiavelli became one of the most widely read and known writers in the European Renaissance ... and also one of the most notorious

After his death in 1527 Machiavelli became one of the most widely read and known writers in the European Renaissance ... and also one of the **most notorious**. *The Prince* was translated into many languages and went into multiple editions, despite being banned in many countries.

As the 'shock value' of his writings began to die away, however, his influence went deeper, taking political thought in **radically new directions**. Nonetheless, his legacy was, and continues to be, contested: was he, at heart, a **democrat and republican**, an apologist for tyrannical regimes or a prophet of **nationalism**, in both its 'good' and 'bad' guises?

Since his death, then, Machiavelli has assumed **multiple identities** – an enduring testament to the **richness** and **depth** of his work.

In this final chapter we will look at:

* Machiavelli's 'Machiavellian' reputation during the Renaissance
* 'Machiavellian' characters in the plays of William Shakespeare
* Machiavelli's relationship to the Italian Risorgimento
* Machiavelli's continuing influence on politics today.

'Machiavellian' Machiavelli

Very soon after his death, Machiavelli became a byword for every kind of **skulduggery**, from deviousness and hypocrisy to irreligiosity and plain simple evil:

> This poison is spread through the courts of princes in this man's books which are circulating almost everywhere.

English cardinal Reginald Pole

> [Machiavelli is] wholly destitute of religion and a condemner thereof.

Churchman Ambrogio Catarino

● During the Renaissance, Machiavelli was often seen as an agent of the devil

Machiavelli was attacked not just by the Catholic Church but also by the new Protestant churches that arose during this time:

✳ In 1559 the Catholic Church included Machiavelli's works on the **first Papal Index of Prohibited Books** because of his 'impiety'.
✳ In 1589 the French Huguenot (Protestant) Innocent Gentillet attacked Machiavelli as an **apologist for tyranny** and as representative of the deviousness of Catholics as a whole. It was the Florentine's diabolical methods, he insisted, that had inspired the Queen Mother at the Catholic French court to carry out the **bloody massacre** of the Huguenots on St Bartholomew's Day in 1572. His theory was given extra mileage because the Queen Mother was none other than Catherine de' Medici, the daughter of Lorenzo de' Medici, to whom Machiavelli had dedicated his most notorious work.

'Murtherous Machevil'

Machiavelli's 'evil' reputation was also widespread in England, where he was closely associated with popular ideas about the **cloak-and-dagger politics** of the Italian princely courts. Although *The Prince* was banned under Elizabeth I and its first English language translation did not appear until 1640, versions in the original Italian as well as in French and Latin were widely read.

The great English playwright **William Shakespeare** (1564–1616) was deeply influenced by the ideas of Machiavelli – like the Italian thinker, he was deeply concerned with how rulers seize, maintain and fall from power, as well as with **'power play'** more generally:

Shakespeare ... like the Italian thinker ... was deeply concerned with how rulers seize, maintain and fall from power ...

Richard III

The most 'Machiavellian' character in Shakespeare is undoubtedly **Richard III**, who schemes, bullies, cajoles and murders his way to power – as shown in *Henry VI*, Part 3 (1590–91) and *Richard II* (1592). In *Henry VI* (Part 3, 3.2) he praises his own mastery of subterfuge, in which he claims to outstrip even Machiavelli:

> I can add colours to the chameleon
> Change shapes with Proteus for advantages
> And set the murtherous Machevil to school
> Can I do this, and cannot get a crown?

* The title character of *Macbeth* (*c*. 1604) shows a military man of *virtù* coming to power by means of 'wickedness' (see Chapter 4) – the murder of King Duncan – and charts the consequent disintegration of his rule.

* In *Othello* (1602–03) Iago adroitly exploits the weaknesses of others in order to manipulate them.

Machiavelli the patriot

A very different image of Machiavelli eventually evolved in Italy, where he came to be seen as a passionate **Italian patriot**.

The final chapter of *The Prince* – an exhortation to a saviour-prince who would rescue Italy from the chaos and misery inflicted on it by invaders – was seen as a call for **a unified Italian state**:

> **'Now Italy, left as if lifeless, awaits the man who may heal her wounds ... and who can cure her of these sores that have been festering for so long. Look how she prays to God to send someone to redeem her from these barbaric cruelties and insults. See how ready she is to follow a banner, provided that someone picks it up.'**

For this reason, during the **Risorgimento** (the 'Resurgence') – the period in the nineteenth century during which Italy was united into a single state – Machiavelli was seen as kind of **figurehead of Italian nationalism**, commemorated in numerous statues and street names across Italy.

Machiavelli and Mussolini

A much darker side of Italian nationalism emerged during the 1920s with the rise of the **fascist dictator Benito Mussolini**. Mussolini saw himself as just that saviour-prince heralded by Machiavelli and, like the Renaissance thinker, looked back to the Roman Republic as a model for a **strong new Italian state**. For Mussolini, *The Prince* was the 'statesman's supreme guide'. More generally, Machiavelli's espousal of strong, amoral government, of masculine *virtù* and of war as the principal tool of statecraft has been seen as a blueprint for **totalitarian regimes** of whatever political hue.

Machiavelli's influence as a political thinker

As we saw in Chapter 3, Machiavelli helped to create a **new dimension** of political thought. Instead of musing about what politics should be in an ideal world, he insisted on grounding it in the realities of human nature and in the pressures of the here and now.

For him the key political question was not so much 'How can we create the best possible political system?' but 'How can we act for the best now, at *this* moment, given *these* circumstances?'

As such, his influence can be seen, for example, in:

* the political philosophy of the English thinker **Thomas Hobbes** (1588–1679), who argued for a strong state in order to quell the natural state of war that would otherwise exist between individuals
* the ethical standpoint known as **utilitarianism**, which argues that acts (including political ones) must be judged not in themselves but for their outcomes (their utility or usefulness).

Realpolitik

The Machiavellian, 'realist' approach to politics later crystallized in the political philosophy of realpolitik, a German term first coined in the nineteenth century and exemplified by the policies of the statesmen Prince Klemens von Metternich and Otto von Bismarck.

The terrifying challenge laid down by Machiavelli in *The Prince* still haunts politics to this day.

* Should our politicians act **for the sake of ideals** – abstract notions of freedom, democracy and human rights – regardless of the consequences?
* Or should they try to act **pragmatically**, being prepared to get their hands dirty if a greater evil is to be avoided?

Further reading

The place to start, of course, is with **Machiavelli's writings** themselves. *The Prince* is Machiavelli at his most accessible, astringent and infuriating – both Oxford World's Classics and Penguin do excellent editions. *The Discourses* provide another accessible, if more time-consuming, read – again both Oxford University Press and Penguin offer good translations with useful introductions and notes. Among his non-political works I would recommend *The Mandrake Root*, although tracking down an English translation may be harder.

For **Machiavelli's life**, there is an excellent recent biography by Miles J. Unger (Simon & Schuster, 2011). For the **historical background**, Christopher Hibbert's *The Rise and Fall of the Medici* (Penguin, re-issue edition, 2001) is hugely enjoyable, although now a little dated. *Death in Florence: The Medici, Savonarola and the Battle for the Soul of the Renaissance City* by Paul Strathern (Jonathan Cape, 2011) is an in-depth account of the crisis years of the Republic.